"In a world where so many peopl
Joshua digs to the bottom of the b
were there all along. *Blessings in Disguise* offers a new perspective
that helps us break our bondage to circumstances and find joy in life
as is really is."

–Ken Davis, *New York Times* Best-selling author, comedian

"Many books are written each year but few challenge your thinking
and elevate your spirit like *Blessings in Disguise*. Joshua will change
the way you look at adversity as he untangles life's problems with
pertinent scriptures and artful illustrations. Get ready to be blessed."

–Jim Laudell
Author of *Highpoints*

"*Blessings in Disguise* lays out the compelling argument for taking a
second look at what we so quickly brand as 'bad luck' through
spiritual eyes. Joshua wastes no time in getting to the beautiful heart
of the matter in this quick read, bound to change the way the reader
looks at their life from now on. A blend of stories and scripture that
beckon another read through!"

–Kim de Blecourt
Orphan rights advocate, and author of
*Until We All Come Home: A Harrowing Journey, a Mother's
Courage, a Race to Freedom*

"Things don't always turn out the way we expect — and that's a
good thing. Joshua will tell you why in this great book about what
life's really about (hint: it's not being comfortable)."

–Jeff Goins
Author of *Wrecked: When a Broken World Slams into Your
Comfortable Life*

"Joshua tackles some of life's most troubling questions about God
and life with candor, faith, and a healthy dose of humor. You won't
put *Blessings in Disguise* down without having something to think
about!"

–Kristy Howard
Blogger, wife, mommy, and author of four books

To my best friend, Jesus. Without you, I am nothing. Thank you for blessing me with burdens. And to my wonderful parents, Gerald and Gwen Hood. I love you both.

Contents

Foreword

Maybe you are like me. I used to believe God had a perfect plan for my life, and I was simply acting out His play. Everything I did, He had already ordained or purposed for me. From my college, career, even my choice of a husband I was just doing my best to follow script.

When I was twenty-two years old and diagnosed with a type of cancer only found in men over the age of eighty, I thanked God for it. I really did! Surely He was using this for ministry, right?

When I was diagnosed with cancer the second time, or experienced the death of my daughter born premature, I thought, "God's in control. He has a plan . . . and somehow, some way, this is just part of it." Even after a miscarriage, I was still humming the same tune . . . albeit a little more hesitantly. And then, my definition of what "God's plans" were shattered into a million pieces.

My husband and I were in the process of adopting a precious baby boy. We named him. We brought him home from the hospital. We fell madly in love. We were so ready to begin our lives as a family. But one unexpected phone call later, we were overcome with devastation. His mother had changed her mind and wanted him back.

At that point, all the well-meaning mentions of, "God has a plan, you need to trust Him!" or, "This was just part of God's plan," and all the "Jeremiah 29:11s" left me furious!

In fact, there were times I wanted to punch people in the face. Yes, I admit it.

How could this be God's plan?

It wasn't until this point in my life when I stopped taking everyone else's definition of "God's plan," and decided to do my own research. I absolutely refused to believe that God was a God who needed lies and manipulation to accomplish His purposes; the very reasons our adoption failed in the first place. So, for the first time in my life, I contemplated God's will versus human decision. Were we able to make our own decisions? Or has God already predestined every detail in our lives, and we are just along for the ride?

Through weeks and months of studying the Bible, talking to pastors, and working through this with people much, much smarter than me, I came to realize there is a big difference between what God plans and what God allows to happen. In the end, I was forced to redefine what "God's plans" really meant.

I began to realize God didn't give me cancer; He allowed me to have cancer. God didn't make my daughter die; He allowed my daughter to die. God didn't force our failed adoption; He allowed it to happen.

This enabled me to understand God and His plans in a whole new way. I began to understand that God's original plan, His original design, was perfection.

There was no sickness, human deception, or death (and a whole host of other consequences), until Adam and Eve made the decision to disobey God and sin. And, because of this one decision, we now live in an imperfect world, where imperfect things will happen.

While I have always believed God is sovereign, I used to think that meant not to question anything that happened in our lives, because "God is God, and I am not!" However, I started to understand that it is because of God's sovereignty that He is able to maintain His goodness and holiness in the face of tragedy—because He planned the consequences to sin; not because He ordained the original sin (or any sin for that matter) to occur. It is because of God's sovereignty that He allows cancer, death, sickness, and other frustrations as consequences of the first sin, for God cannot plan such evil.

And lastly, I learned only God can bring good out of tragedy! Only He can take our greatest trials, disappointments, failures, and even sins, and turn them into something that will bring Him glory! This is not something we can do on our own, and it is the very promise of Romans 8:28.

Because of our personal tragedies, I have seen God use our pain to build rapport with others who have experienced similar hurts. This rapport led to an entire Grief Ministry— something I never would have asked for, yet a place where we are finding purpose in our trials. Because of the worst days of our lives, we can now help men and women understand they are not alone and equip people to effectively help the hurting through their own worst days.

If we are to live crazy, as Joshua suggests in this book, we must examine our perspective of how God is working in and through our lives when hurts and tragedy strike.

Absorb Joshua's words, and let them sink in, even if all you can see right now are the tearstained pillows and your shattered plans. God is there, and your hurt is not going unnoticed by Him!

- Erica McNeal, author of Good Grief!
@toddanderica
www.ericamcneal.com

"And we know that all things work together for good to them that love God, to them who are the called according to his purpose."

—Romans 8:28

1

If I Could Write the Story

I don't know if you do this, but as I'm sitting at the airport gate and waiting on my flight to leave, I always look around to see who's flying with me. I'm not sure exactly what I'm looking for. Explosives hanging out of someone's shirtsleeve, I guess. Despite the wonderful high-tech security measures of modern airports, I still want to see for myself if there's any suspicious-looking activity among the people on my flight.

So before a recent flight from New York City to Dallas, I was giving everybody in the gate area a good once-over. I didn't see any terrorists, but I did spot a beautiful college girl. She was my age and she was absolutely gorgeous.

Being a single, blue-blooded American man, I could not help but notice the good looks God had blessed her with.

She didn't seem to speak English and the few words I'd heard her say sounded like French. I don't speak French. But I thought, *You know what? I could learn.*

She wasn't wearing a ring, and appeared to be traveling alone. Maybe she needed someone to talk to. So I prayed again. *God, she probably needs someone to share the Gospel with her. I am just a willing vessel, Lord. Use me.*

As we boarded the plane, I examined my ticket to see which seat I was in. Up ahead of me, the French girl had already settled into hers. And to my great joy, the seat beside her was— gasp—empty! My heart was pounding in my throat as I reached her row and compared the seat number with my ticket. And you'll never believe it . . .

It didn't match.

My shoulders slumped as I trudged down the aisle and found my seat. My heart was broken and my dreams were shattered. On the bright side though, there were two empty seats beside me. At least I wouldn't have to ride for three hours crammed beside other people.

I decided to have a good attitude about the whole thing. I spread out, pulled out my iPod, and settled in for the flight. But a few moments later, to my dismay, some last-minute passengers boarded. I watched in horror as a woman and her two screaming children made their way down the aisle. And you'll never guess which seats they had.

Yep. Right beside me.

The woman was Asian and didn't appear to speak English, so I pretended to be asleep.

As soon as we lifted off the runway, her kids went wild. They began shouting, fighting, jumping around, throwing their toys and books, and crying. The most amazing part was their mom didn't even seem to notice. Apparently this was normal for them.

Everyone in the plane began turning around and staring at us, trying to see what all the commotion was about. I shook my head and scowled at the children along with everyone else, to identify that I did not know them and they did not belong to me.

Not only did this lady not spank her children; not only did she not quiet them down; and not only did she fail to even notice them . . . but she promptly fell asleep! In her restful state of quiet bliss, her head slowly dropped until it was resting on my shoulder.

I was frozen in terror for a few seconds. Screaming children were at my feet, their sleeping mother was asleep on my shoulder, and angry looks were being directed my way from all the other passengers.

I couldn't take it anymore. I coughed and shook my shoulder a little more violently than necessary. She jerked awake and looked around.

I smiled contentedly and pressed play on my iPod.

Twenty seconds later, she was asleep on my shoulder again. She drooled on my shirt all the way to Dallas.

***

I sometimes picture life as a book. It begins at our birth as a volume of empty pages. Each day we live is etched into the pages as the story of our life unfolds. And I have learned that *if I were writing my life story, it would look very different.*

Had I been writing my story that day, I would not have been sitting by the sleepy lady with the wild kids. I'd have been six rows ahead, sitting beside the beautiful French girl.

Imagine if you had total control over your life. What if you could write what was going to happen this next week?

Perhaps you would pencil in a promotion on the job. Maybe you'd write some peace into a turbulent relationship. Maybe you'd create a troubling situation to get revenge on someone who hurt your feelings.

But thankfully, and by God's mercy, we don't control our lives. And even though it may not seem like it, that's a good thing.

If you've lived any length of time, you know life doesn't always go the way you would have written it.

While we don't always appreciate it when our prayers aren't answered the way we'd like and plans don't seem as clear or as fair as we had hoped, there's always someone looking out for our best interests.

This little book you're reading is about what to do when life doesn't go like you'd planned.

Oh, *That's* Not Good!

Let me ask you a question. Consider it very carefully. Don't just read the words—think about their meaning, and answer the question clearly in your mind: *What circumstances in your life right now would you call "bad"?*

Maybe it's a health condition. The doctor walked in and rocked your world with three little words: "You have cancer." Or maybe a heart attack left you flat on your back saying, "Oh, *that's* not good."

Maybe it's a financial need. You lost your job and you sit at a kitchen table littered with bills and invoices, running your fingers through your hair, and thinking, "Oh, *that's* not good."

Maybe it's a strained relationship. A friendship you never thought would fall apart did. A marriage you thought was strong wasn't. Your heart is broken, your cheeks are tear-stained, and you're crying out, "Oh, *that's* not good!"

But maybe it's not health, finances, or relational issues that are making you unhappy. Maybe it's something else. Whatever it is, it's the part of your life that would not have been written this way if *you* were writing the story.

We look at these parts of our lives and label them "bad." But I've discovered you and I are *terrible* at evaluating what is good or bad.

I learned this a few years ago when I bought a bass guitar. I found an amazing "scratch-and-dent" deal online and purchased it. When it was delivered to my house a few days later, I tore open the packaging and examined the shiny, glossy, red guitar with awe. I couldn't find a scratch or dent on it anywhere. It played like a dream. I was ecstatic!

This is good! I thought.

But the third time I tried to play it, it wouldn't make a sound. The mechanical pickups were totally dead. "Oh, *that's* not good," I groaned in disappointment.

I called up the company I had bought it from and listened to a five-minute flute solo while waiting for the next available customer service specialist. A few minutes later, a lady answered and I explained the situation. She cheerfully informed me it was probably covered under warranty and she could get it replaced. This fantastic bit of news cheered me up considerably. *This is good!* I thought.

She placed me on hold again, and I listened to more flute music while she checked the order. When she came back on the line she said, "This was a scratch-and-dent item, and unfortunately, it was the only one we had. So I can't replace it with one like it."

I knew it had been too good to be true. I sank down into my chair. *Oh, that's not good,* I groaned to myself.

But before I could respond, she added, "Since we don't have a scratch-and-dent to replace it with, I'll just have to send you a brand new one. Is that okay?"

Is that okay? I thought. *Of course it's okay! This is good!*

Immediately I was in a great mood.

They sent me a brand-new guitar and it is still working perfectly to this day.

When the bass stopped working and I realized there was a problem, my first reaction was, "That's not good!"

But now that I'm on the other side of the problem; now that I've traded it in; and now that I know I ended up with an unbelievable deal . . . I realize it wasn't bad at all.

In fact, what I had labeled bad was actually the best possible thing that could have happened.

And if I could go back, knowing what I know now, as soon as my bass quit working, I would have been excited!

***

I asked you earlier what you would label as "bad." Consider this: Maybe you are labeling those things bad because you are not to the end of the story yet.

Right now, when you look at your pocket book, or when Satan is battling you spiritually, or when you're frustrated with a relationship in your life, your reaction is, "Oh, *that's* not good!" And you label it as a bad thing.

But what if the circumstance you're facing isn't a bad thing at all? What if you discovered the amazing message of Romans 8:28 and realized *all things* work together for good? It would change the way you view your problems forever.

***

A woman was painting the kitchen of her newly acquired country home when she accidentally submerged her left foot in a tray of fresh paint. A few minutes later, as she took off her comfortable, hole-in-the-toe painting shoes, she regretted that she hadn't brought along another pair of socks. She would have to sport a "Country Orange" big toe in her sandals when she picked up her four little sons from the babysitter.

When she arrived, the babysitter told her the kids were still napping, and suggested she do a little shopping and stop back for them later. She didn't get an offer like that very often, so she wasted no time in heading for the department store.

At the store, she quickly made her way to the house wares department and she found that all things really do "work together for good." Because she had stepped in paint earlier, she was able to perfectly match the new kitchen dish cloths and towels to her "Country Orange" toe.

She had labeled her orange toe bad because it wasn't part of her plan, and she didn't know the end of the story. But God had a better plan, and by the end of the story, she saw that her inconvenience was actually a blessing.

When something "bad" happens in our life, our natural response is to get discouraged and think, *This wasn't how I planned it. I wouldn't have written it this way.*

In these times, the inconvenience is often more than a painted toe. And we may not just be left with a broken instrument. We may be left with a broken heart.

But even when the pain is deep, and even when the circumstances are confusing, we don't have to be dismayed. In fact, if we could learn to filter everything through Romans 8:28, we'd have a totally different attitude. We may not see how it's going to work out yet. But Romans 8:28 is a constant reminder that our burdens are actually blessings in disguise.

Understanding That We Don't Understand

What if I told you that yesterday a man knocked me out and cut my skull open with a knife? You would consider that bad, right?

But what if I told you I had brain cancer, the man was a doctor, and he was performing a life-saving operation on me? You would call that good, right?

In one sentence, we went from calling the above scenario "bad" to "good," simply because we learned new information. The fact is that sometimes the things we think are endangering our life are actually the things that are saving it.

The only reason we call any situation in our lives "bad" is because we have limited information. But God knows the rest of the story. Sometimes He'll share it with us. Sometimes He won't. But He put Romans 8:28 in the Bible as a promise that it's all working for our good.

So what are you calling bad? What areas are you looking at and saying, *This is such a battle! This is so hard . . . so difficult . . . this is not the way I want it to be . . .* ?

One of the areas in which we often feel this way is relationships. You can probably think of a relationship in your life that isn't the way you wish it was.

Maybe your father left you as a child. Every day you discover new fragments of your heart you didn't even realize were broken. Every day you struggle beneath a load of bitterness and hurt. And just when you think you've forgotten or forgiven, it resurfaces yet again.

Maybe your relationship with a family member has become strained. You're not even sure what went wrong, but feelings were hurt and communication became infrequent. You're not sure if things will ever be the same again.

Maybe you don't get along with a coworker. You dread seeing them at work. They talk about you behind your back. You want to show them the love of Christ, but it's a daily struggle.

Maybe it's a relationship with someone at church that is anything but peaceful and perfect. In fact, it's a constant struggle and burden. You're discouraged, frustrated, and disappointed.

But I want to challenge you to understand that what you're calling bad may be the best thing that could happen to you. God may be using the struggle and pain of that relationship for your good and His glory in amazing ways you can't see.

I know it requires a pretty big leap of faith to believe that. Especially when all we see is the struggle, pain, and frustration. But the Bible challenges us to:

> "Trust in the Lord with all your heart,
> and lean not on your own understanding."
> (Proverbs 3:5)

Lean not on what? On your own understanding. On *what you know.*

When my bass stopped working, all I knew was I had a broken instrument. I didn't know the company was going to send me a brand new one. I didn't know it was going to work out better than I could have ever expected. All I knew was I had brokenness.

And maybe you're in the same place. You're holding brokenness. You don't see how it's going to be put back together. You don't see the answer. But if you'll trust in the Lord with all your heart, you *don't have to know* how it's going to work out.

That's an amazing relief!

2

Why God Doesn't Answer Your Prayers

Have you ever wanted something God wouldn't let you have? Have you ever felt like God was holding out on you? I have.

Satan tries to make us feel this way all the time. In fact, it's one of his oldest tricks, and dates all the way back to the Garden of Eden.

God created Adam and Eve and placed them in the most beautiful environment you could ever imagine. Don't let the term "garden" fool you. We're not talking cornstalks and tomato plants here. We're talking Hawaii, Jamaica, Fiji, and Tuscany all rolled into one. Breathtaking views on every side. Beautiful sunsets every evening. Perfect climate all year round. No mosquito bites. Seriously, what more could you ask for?

Well, that's exactly the question Satan got Eve to focus on.

She and Adam were surrounded by every kind of amazing vegetation you could imagine. Beautiful-smelling bouquets of flowers in all colors. Crisp apples, juicy oranges, and a million other varieties growing all around.

God gestures toward the Garden with a sweep of His hand and says to Adam and Eve, "Here you go! It's all for your enjoyment. Smell the flowers, savor the flavors of the fruit, and play with the beautiful animals. Enjoy!"

Then He adds one more tiny detail. "Oh, by the way, I placed one little tree over here that I'd like you to avoid, please."

Now let's press pause right there.

When you've created thousands of acres of luscious enjoyment for Adam and Eve, asking them to avoid a single tree is no big deal. But why bother? Why create the opportunity for rebellion?

The answer is powerful: the presence of that tree freed them from slavery. Without it, there would have been no opportunity to disobey. And with no opportunity to disobey, Adam and Eve would be nothing more than robots. They would love God because there was no other option. They would obey God merely because there was no alternative. They would be nothing more than slaves.

But because God gave them a choice, they had the option of loving Him from their hearts. The existence of a tree they couldn't have was a blessing that made true love possible.

Satan obviously didn't want them to see what a blessing this was. So he told Eve that God was holding out on her. (Pay close attention here!) Up until this point, Eve's perception of God was a loving creator who provided what she needed.

Satan wants to change this perception. So for the first time in history, he paints a picture of God as an unjust, jealous, and cruel deity. Thousands of years later, Satan is still doing the same thing. He whispers things like:

"Why did God let your children die in that car wreck? How could He love you?"

"Why won't God let you get married? You'd be so much happier."

"How could God let your business fail? He wants other people to be successful, but not you?"

There are many lessons we can learn from Genesis 3. But one of the most important is this: what we don't have is a blessing.

The most beautiful thing Adam and Eve could experience was a true, non-obligatory love relationship with God. And the one thing they couldn't have made their greatest blessing possible. Had

God not placed that tree there, they could have never truly loved Him.

Could it be that the forbidden tree in your life is what is making your greatest blessings possible? Could it be that the circumstances that make God seem unjust are actually blessings in disguise?

God knows exactly what He's doing. And He has promised you that in His love, He is working all things in your life for your good. Even the things you can't have.

But like Adam and Eve, we often long for "blessings" that would actually be burdens if God gave them to us.

I bet there's a "forbidden tree" in your life. What are you longing for that you feel like God won't give you?

Listen to what these two verses from Psalms say:

"For the LORD God is a sun and shield: the LORD will give grace and glory:
no good thing will he withhold from them that walk uprightly."
(Psalm 84:11, emphasis mine)

"The young lions suffer want and hunger;
but *those who seek the Lord lack no good thing.*"
(Psalm 34:10, emphasis mine)

Those words are simply staggering and they've rocked my world more than once. They say if I am walking uprightly, God will not withhold a single good thing from me.

The only logical conclusion then, is if I'm living right and there's something I want but don't have, it means it would not be a good thing for me to have it!

This is where our ideas and God's ideas collide because at any given time in our lives, there are a lot of things we'd like to have that we don't. And in our opinion, it sure seems like life would be better if we had these things. So it takes a ton of faith to trust that it wouldn't. But it's necessary if you're going to be able to get past the temporary pains of not having what you desire.

Maybe you have longed for healing, a job, a wife, or a baby. You have earnestly prayed for weeks and months—even years. But you are still sick, still unemployed, still single, and still childless.

And you are disappointed. Like Adam and Eve, you want that one thing it seems like God won't give you.

But you know God promises that those who seek Him will lack no good thing. Which means, if something is good, God will give it to you.

That's hard to swallow. After all, you are still sick, unemployed, single, and childless.

So what do we do when God promises to give us everything that's good, but we long for things we don't have? The only way to answer that question is to understand what is truly *good.*

We're going to dive much deeper into this in the last chapter, but for now, listen to what Paul says in Philippians 3:8:

> "…I count all things but loss for the excellency of the knowledge of Christ…"

That's a pretty strong statement. He's saying *nothing* is more important or valuable than getting to know God better. So if God is our greatest good, then what makes something good is whether it brings us more of God.

So if God is withholding something in your life right now (healing, a job, a wife, children, or anything else), you are not lacking any good thing because God has ordained the longing for that thing to bring you more of Himself. And having more of Him is the best thing that could happen to you. Ever.

What God wants for you is better than what you want for you.

When I feel disappointed by God, it's because at that moment there's something I'm longing for more than Him. And as good as healing, employment, marriage, and children are, none of them will ever come close to satisfying me as much as God will.

I Want to Be Rich

Though we don't realize it, many of the things we long for would harm us, not help us. That's why Jesus said it would be difficult for rich people to make it into heaven. Some of us may want a spouse, job, or baby, but we *all* want money. We all think it would be a good thing if we had more of it.

And I don't know about you, but I think I could handle wealth. I think I'd be smart and generous with it. You probably feel the same way. And if you asked your friends, they probably feel the same way, too.

But the truth is, despite our high opinion of ourselves, very few of us could handle abundant wealth. The majority of people who encounter sudden wealth go bankrupt, get divorced, and have family feuds. At least seventy percent of them squander away all their money. For almost 100 percent of them, every bit of their wealth is gone by the third generation.

The money seems like a dream come true. But their dream quickly turns into a nightmare.

When you have that kind of money, everyone is suddenly your friend. Everyone wants a piece of the pie. It's hard to tell what people's true motives are anymore. Every organization and cause in the world wants a donation.

"But they that will be rich fall into temptation and a snare,
and into many foolish and hurtful lusts,
which drown men in destruction and perdition."
(1 Timothy 6:9)

Ouch. Even having read all that, you probably still want wealth. So do I. And wealth is not always a bad thing. But only God knows what it would do to us. Only He knows the effects it would have on our life.

No good thing will He withhold. Believing that requires an enormous amount of trust. And trust is really what it all comes down to.

God's Word promises us as Christians that if we don't have something, it means that God, in His all-powerful and all-knowing perspective, has chosen not to give us that thing because it would harm us, not help us. (You might want to read that sentence again.)

That's easy to accept when God's plan matches our own. But what about when we are stuck on the side of the road with a flat tire? We didn't plan on that. But God did. And our plans didn't match.

That's when it's hard to believe Psalm 84:11. How could that be good? Why could God not have let us get safely to work on time? Look at the ninth word of that verse again:

"For the LORD God is a sun and *shield* . . ."
(Psalm 84:11, emphasis mine)

God has abundantly lavished blessings on our lives. But the crazy thing is, we never even see the vast majority of those blessings. Just as the tip of the iceberg is all that's visible above the ocean's surface, all the blessings we are aware of make up a small portion of God's actual goodness to us. The majority of our blessings lie hidden beneath the ocean of flat tires, accidents, and all of life's other unplanned inconveniences.

Could that flat tire have prevented us from being in a fatal accident further down the road? Had we arrived at work on time, could we have seen something or heard something God knew we didn't need to see or hear? Could it be that the Lord God was being a shield for us just like Psalm 84:11 says?

I experienced this firsthand while traveling down the interstate on a business trip one day. I was overcome by a strange feeling that I needed to pull over at the next exit. I didn't really need anything and I was in a hurry to get to my destination. But I had never had a feeling like this before. It was so real and strong that I pulled over anyway. I got out and stretched my legs at a gas station for a few minutes until the feeling went away.

When I pulled back onto the interstate and crested a hill, a massive car wreck had just occurred—cars rolling, metal flying, glass breaking. Overturned cars were scattered in the median. It had happened only seconds before.

Immediately, I realized why I had felt the sudden and unexplainable need to pull over. The Lord God was being my shield. And I have no doubt my inconvenient pit-stop saved me from tragedy. It wasn't a burden. It was a blessing in disguise.

Maybe you think it was just coincidence. But I don't. I think it was Psalm 84:11 in action. And you can probably tell stories of your own just like it.

So let's not be so quick to be like a small child who is complaining of a scratched hand after just been tackled out of the way of an oncoming car.

Some of God's greatest blessings in your life are the times He has messed up your plans. Maybe you should write that down and stick it on your refrigerator, on your desk, or in your car. That way, when things don't go the way you planned and you're tempted to label something bad, you can remember this truth.

God doesn't mess up your plans out of vengeance or spite. He does it out of mercy.

***

In the aftermath of the terrorist attacks on September 11, 2001, amazing stories began to surface about life-saving inconveniences.

Once man survived because his son started kindergarten that day.

Another fellow was alive because it was his turn to bring donuts.

One woman was late because her alarm clock didn't go off in time.

One was late because of being stuck on the New Jersey Turnpike due to an auto accident.

One man missed his bus.

One spilled food on her clothes and had to take time to change.

One's car wouldn't start.

One couldn't find a taxi.

Another guy put on a new pair of shoes that morning. On his way to work, he developed a blister on his foot. What an inconvenience! He stopped at a drugstore to buy a Band-Aid and that's why he's alive today.

So when you're stuck in traffic, miss an elevator, turn back to answer a ringing telephone, or encounter any of the other little things that annoy you, stop and remind yourself, *This is exactly where God wants me to be at this very moment.*

And the next time your morning seems to be going wrong, the children are slow getting dressed, you can't seem to find the car keys, or you hit every traffic light, don't get mad or frustrated. It may just be that God is at work watching over you.

Let's not be so quick to label inconveniences as bad. Let's not be so quick to dread flat tires, sick days, bad news, and schedule changes. In His great love, God might just be shielding us. And chances are, they're not burdens at all. They're blessings in disguise.

May God continue to bless us with all those annoying little things. And may we remember their possible purpose.

Why God Not Answering Your Prayer Is a Good Thing

What have you been praying for lately?

Your prayers reveal your plan. You pray according to the way *you* would write the story.

For example, we pray for health, because that's how we'd like the story to read. We pray for no pain and no problems. All our prayers are for God to run our lives the way we would run them. We never ask God to do things in a way we wouldn't do them. (Have you ever noticed that?)

So what you are asking God for reveals what you think is ahead and how you would like things to turn out. And God may do it that way. If He does—great!

But you are in situations now, and will continue to be, where life's not going to happen the way you would've written it out. And so many people get tripped up when their experience doesn't match their expectation.

They expect God to do something, and He doesn't. They get confused and disillusioned. Their experience (how things went), didn't match their expectation (how they expected things to go).

I'm not just writing this book to tell you God can work out all your problems, although that's great news in and of itself. I have even better news: The fact that those problems are in your life is a blessing. I know that's hard to believe. But it's true. And you will attain a whole new level of joy when you realize God isn't just going to raise the dead—the fact that Lazarus died is a *good thing!*

We often marvel when we think God has rescued a bad situation. But God wants us to marvel that He had it planned all along, and it wasn't even a bad situation to begin with!

But we don't naturally think that way. We're human. We lean on our own understanding. And so we pray according to *our* plan.

With that in mind, look at the two verses that come right *before* Romans 8:28:

"Likewise the Spirit also helpeth our infirmities:
for we know not what we should pray for as we ought:
but the Spirit itself maketh intercession for us with groanings which cannot be uttered.
And he that searcheth the hearts knoweth what is the mind of the Spirit,
because he maketh intercession for the saints according to the will of God."
(Romans 8:26–27, emphasis mine)

The truth is, we don't even know how to pray most of the time. And sometimes when we pray for something, God loves us enough to not answer our prayer.

Have you ever prayed for something, only to look back later and be glad God didn't answer your prayer?

Oh wow, God. I'm glad You didn't let me marry that woman. I'm glad You didn't let me take that job.

We can say that now. But back when we didn't know the rest of the story, we were saying, "Lord, I think you should write the book this way . . ."

Now that we see how God worked it all out for our good, we can look back and applaud His work.

God, You did good. I'm glad You didn't answer my prayer. I'm glad You didn't write that chapter the way I wanted You to.

Only once we can see the past with the benefit of hindsight do we realize our unanswered prayer was a blessing in disguise.

Being a Christian doesn't mean you won't face things or nothing will ever go wrong. In fact, 2 Timothy 3:12 says,

" . . . all who live Godly in Christ Jesus shall suffer persecution."

So there's going to be pain. There are going to be problems. There are going to be many times you wouldn't have written your life the way it turns out. But in those times, God is working in ways that you won't see until later.

You can probably look back over your life and say, *Isn't it good that God did this, or worked this out, or led me to this* . . . And the reason you're able to do that is because you're on *this* side of the storm.

But for some reason, when we're on the *other* side of the storm and we look ahead, we doubt and fear. *I don't know how this is going to turn out. What should I do about this decision?*

Maybe I'm radical. But I am just crazy enough to believe that it is God's will for us to live the same way on both sides of the storm if *all* things truly work together for good. And they do.

Let me be clear: I'm not advocating that everything is good. I'm advocating that God *works all things together* for good. There's a big difference.

Cancer is not a good thing. But the amazing message of Romans 8:28, and the amazing thing about our God, is that He can take bad things (like cancer) and use them for good.

Having to have heart surgery is not a good thing. But God works it for good.

Losing a loved one is not a good thing. But God works it for good.

Abuse and pain and heartache are not good things. But God works them for good.

Isn't He amazing?

Because the Bible promises God will work all things together for good, there is no need to be discouraged on this side of the storm. I truly believe we can maintain the same attitude, joy, and peace on this side of the storm before God works it out, as we can on the other side after He works it out. It doesn't change the way He blesses us but it sure changes the amount of stress we create for ourselves.

And instead of being discouraged when God doesn't answer our prayers, we will realize He is doing what is best for us.

3

But If Not

Nobody has ever grown up thinking, "I'm going to be in a terrible car accident at age thirty-one."

Life constantly keeps us off balance with unexpected twists and turns. And it's not just *sometimes* that things don't go the way we want. *Most of the time* they don't. We spend the majority of our life in uncharted waters we didn't plan on swimming in.

Now all of this is easy to talk about. We can throw around all kinds of clichés and cute phrases about how when life gives us lemons we just need to make lemonade. But what about when the rubber meets the road? What about when life spirals out of control?

What do you do with a shattered dream? What do you do with an unmet expectation? What do you do when you have a heart attack, lose your job, or a relationship falls apart? What do you do when tears are streaming down your face, your heart is crushed, and you don't know how the story's going to end? When you have more questions than answers and your life is falling apart, cute clichés just aren't going to cut it.

I don't have all the answers. But the Bible does, and it tells us there are four things we need to know when life falls apart. The last one we'll talk about in chapter seven. But before I tell you the others, let me introduce you to three strapping young fellows who have experienced the unexpected free-falls of life's rollercoaster.

Their names are Hannaniah, Mishael, and Azariah. You probably know them as Shadrach, Meshach, and Abednego (or "Shadrach, Radio Shack, and to bed we go" as one four-year-old mistakenly quoted).

You're probably familiar with the story of the egotistical king named Nebuchadnezzar who constructed a gigantic golden statue and informed everyone they had the choice of bowing down and worshipping it, or marinating in a fire-pit. Friendly fellow, this Nebuchadnezzar.

Shadrach, Meshach, and Abednego knew worshipping a golden statue was first of all, stupid, and more importantly, displeasing to God. It would've been easy to quickly scrape a knee against the pavement. (Lesson one: Doing the wrong thing is almost always easier than doing the right thing.) But they were men of strong principle and sturdy character. They refused and stood tall.

The next thing they know, they're standing before an angry king and a hot oven. (Lesson two: good decisions aren't always immediately rewarded.)

Nebuchadnezzar goes over everything with them again: music plays, you bow, I don't roast you. (Lesson three: Satan will always give you a second chance to make a mistake.)

And it is then that these three men make one of the most epic statements of faith in human history:

"If it be so, our God whom we serve is able to deliver us from the burning fiery furnace,
and he will deliver us out of thine hand, O king.
But if not, be it known unto thee, O king, that we will not serve thy gods,
nor worship the golden image which thou hast set up."
(Daniel 3:17–18)

To paraphrase, they said, "God is powerful enough to keep this bad thing from happening. That's what we'd like. That's how we'd write it. But if not . . . "

But if not. Those epic words are an anthem of faith that still echo today.

God can work everything out the way I want. *But if not*, I still trust Him.

God can prevent or heal disease. *But if not*, I will still trust Him.

God can restore this relationship. *But if not*, I will still trust Him.

God can prosper my business. *But if not*, I will still trust Him.

My faith isn't dependent on perfect circumstances or fairytale endings. My faith is in a God who is the same yesterday, today, and forever. He is in control. He knows what He's doing. And though He slay me, yet will I trust Him.

The fiery furnace may look like disaster to me. But Romans 8:28 promises me it's a blessing in disguise.

God Is With You

> "Then Nebuchadnezzar the king was astonished,
> and rose up in haste, and spake,
> and said unto his counselors,
> Did not we cast three men bound into the midst of the fire?
> They answered and said unto the king, True, O king.
> He answered and said, Lo, I see four men loose,
> walking in the midst of the fire,
> and they have no hurt; and the form of the fourth
> is like the Son of God."
> (Daniel 3:24–25)

There is never a moment of your life when God is not right there with you. You will never face a problem without Him. You will never enter a fire alone. He has promised that He will never leave you, nor forsake you (Hebrews 13:5). And when God makes a promise, He keeps it.

He is not going to jump ship. He is not going to give up and bail out of your life. He is not going to pull a disappearing act. You are His bride and "divorce" does not exist in His vocabulary.

When you're happy, He's there. When you're sad, He's there. On the good days and on the bad days. When things are going right and when things are going wrong.

He is always, always, always going to be there.

God Is In Control

Let those four little words rattle around in your mind: God is in control.

No matter what's going on in your life right now, He's in control.

No matter what your problems are. No matter what your finances are. No matter how impossible or discouraging things may seem. No matter what the economy does. No matter how poor your health is. No matter what you gain or what you lose. No matter how good things get. No matter how bad things get.

In triumph and tragedy, elation and desperation, He's in control. That's where our peace comes from. Things may not be going according to *your* plan. But they're still going according to His.

If you struggle with relinquishing control, you're not alone. It is tough. And like forgiveness, it's not just a decision you make once—when hard times arise, you have to constantly remind yourself that you're not in control and that it's okay to let go of your expectations, your fears, and your disappointments. There have been millions who struggled with this through history and there will be millions more. You're in good company.

With that in mind, let the words of this old hymn sink into your soul:

I don't know about tomorrow;
I just live from day to day.
I don't borrow from its sunshine
For its skies may turn to grey.
I don't worry o'er the future,
For I know what Jesus said.
And today I'll walk beside Him,
For He knows what lies ahead.

I don't know about tomorrow;
It may bring me poverty.
But the one who feeds the sparrow,
Is the one who stands by me.
And the path that is my portion
May be through the flame or flood;
But His presence goes before me
And I'm covered with His blood.

Many things about tomorrow
I don't seem to understand
But I know who holds tomorrow
And I know who holds my hand.

("I Know Who Holds Tomorrow," © Ira Stanphill)

God's Way Is Best

When a lay preacher and a nurse discovered their otherwise healthy son was born without arms and legs, they didn't know what to do. They cried. They prayed. The traveled to all kinds of doctors and specialists, but to no avail.

As little Nick grew up, it quickly became evident to him that he was not like the other kids. They laughed at him when he placed his forehead on the ground to wriggle himself upright. They began to bully him.

He became more and more depressed. How could he ever get a job? How could any woman ever love a man with no arms or legs? He would simply be a burden to all those around him for the rest of his life.

Things finally seemed so hopeless that he tried to commit suicide. Thankfully, he failed.

His life began to change for the better as he learned God had a perfect plan for him, and being born without limbs was a part of it. God was not punishing him. In fact, his disability was a tool God could use to change the world.

Today, Nick Vujicic is married, owns several businesses, is a best-selling author, and travels the globe telling people that God is in control. He has spoken to over four million people, and has led thousands to Christ. You might have even heard him speak or seen one of his YouTube videos.

His life has impacted far more people on this earth than it would have had he been born with arms and legs. God had a better plan for his life than he could have ever had for himself. And it certainly wasn't the same life that Nick would have written if he were in charge.

***

That's an inspiring story and you've probably heard lots of others like it. But do you really believe God has the power to do that in *your* life?

Nick can look back on his life now and see that everything turned out great.

So could Shadrach, Meshach, and Abednego.

You have to imagine they were pretty excited when it was all said and done, because when the dust settled, the only thing they lost in the fire was their shackles. Nebuchadnezzar was worshipping God, made a law that everyone in the entire kingdom had to worship Him too, and promoted Shadrach, Meshach, and Abednego.

Had things gone the way they would have written it, none of those amazing things would have happened. God's plan was better. *Way* better.

Had things gone the way Nick would have written it, none of the amazing events and impact of his life would have happened either. God's plan was better. *Way* better.

And despite our stubborn clinging to it, if we will abandon our silly little script, we'll discover that God has amazing things in store for us, too. Things that would never be possible if things went the way we planned.

Don't miss out on the amazing story God has planned for your life.

Now that you understand why His ways are better, this verse is worth reading again:

"Trust in the Lord with all your heart,
and lean not on your own understanding."
(Proverbs 3:5)

When we question our circumstances, we are saying we are smarter than God.

"No God, You don't understand! If You don't heal Lazarus, he's going to die!"

"No God, You don't understand! If You don't make the king have mercy on us, he's going to throw us in the fiery furnace!"

"No God, You don't understand! If You don't give me arms and legs, I'll never be able to accomplish anything!"

How silly are we? It's astoundingly prideful and arrogant of us to think we know better than God. He knows the ending from the beginning. He already knows every tiny detail about the entire rest of our lives!

When we are whining about how things aren't going the way we want, God is sadly shaking His head saying, "You don't understand, child. I have amazing things in store for you. My plan is better. *Way* better. Trust Me."

4

Living Crazy

In the fourth chapter of 2 Kings, the Bible tells us of a woman who cares about the prophet Elisha so much that she and her husband added a little room off the back of their garage for him to stay in whenever he is in town.

She has never been able to have children and longs to be a parent. God rewards the couple's kindness to Elisha by blessing them with a son. The little guy is the joy and delight of their lives.

But tragically one morning, he begins to complain of a headache, and dies a few hours later. She lays him on Elisha's bed in the room behind the garage and shuts the door. Then she hitches up a donkey and tears across the countryside toward Mount Carmel where Elisha is staying at that time.

Now keep in mind, this little lady has been living right. She is a loving wife to her husband. She is a loving mother to her precious son. She cooks and cleans and even adds a room to the house for the prophet. She's doing everything she knows is right.

And what does she get for it? The one thing most precious to her in the world is taken away. And now she is left with brokenness.

Have you ever felt that way? Have you ever felt that you didn't deserve your problems?

Maybe you want a child so badly, but can't have one. You'd give anything to be a mother or a father. And everywhere you look you see other people having children. People who won't be near as good a parent as you would be. People who didn't even want to get pregnant. People who won't love their child like you would love yours.

What did you do to deserve this?

Maybe your business is struggling. You run it by Christian principles and work long hours, but it seems like you just can't make a profit. In the meantime, you're surrounded by greedy crooks who are raking in tons of money and enjoying wild success.

What did you do to deserve this?

Maybe you long to be married. You dream of finding your soul mate. But instead, the ache of loneliness is your constant companion. You're financially, emotionally, and spiritually prepared for married life. Yet everywhere you look, you see immature couples getting engaged. Cupid's arrows seem to be striking everyone except you.

What did you do to deserve this?

These situations don't seem fair, do they? They feel so unjust. But before we go down that road, let's hit the pause button for a second, because this is a crucial point in our lives.

What do we do when God doesn't make sense and life isn't fair? Well, there are a few options.

Some people blame God: "How could God let this happen?"

Some people question God: "Why does God let bad things happen to good people?"   Some people grow bitter against God: "If that's how God rolls, I want no part of Him."

The lady in 2 Kings could have reacted in any of these ways. But she had an understanding of this Romans 8:28 principle long before Romans was ever written.

Elisha asks her, "Is everything okay? Is everything good?" He also specifically asks, "Is it well with the child?"

Now I'm going to be real with you here. If it had been me, I'd have screamed, "You better believe it's *not* well! I'm trying to serve God. I'm doing everything I know that's right. I'm working as hard as I can. And the one thing I treasure most is gone. No. It's *not* good."

But she said *yes!*

We've read the rest of the story. We know what happens. But she didn't. So think about her response. (By the way, if you don't know the end of the story, check out 2 Kings 4. You'll love it.)

Now if you back up and look at it, I would say that woman was crazy. If you find me at the funeral home and my two-year-old is in the casket, I'm not going to be saying, "It's good." That literally sounds crazy!

But that's what the Christian life is all about. That's what Jesus came to call us to—living with crazy faith because of God's promise that He'll work it all out for good.

And she wasn't the only one who had crazy faith. The Bible is full of people who believed in God's faithfulness even though they had no proof of what the outcome would be.

God: "Abraham, this is God. I want you to leave everything and go to the land I will show you."

Abraham: "Whoa, wait . . . what? You want me to move? I've lived here my whole life."

God: "I know."

Abraham: "I can't just pack up on the spur of the moment, march off into the desert, and leave everything I've ever known!"

God: "Why not?"

Abraham: "I don't know . . . because it's crazy!"

God: "Guess what else?"

Abraham: "Oh boy. What?"

God: "I'm going to make you the father of a great nation."

Abraham: "Ha! Impossible. I don't have any kids."

God: "I know. Just trust me."

Abraham: "Okay, let me see if I've got this straight. You want me to leave everything I have, travel into the desert with no idea where I'm going, and become the father of a great nation? Is this some kind of joke? What am I supposed to tell my wife?"

God: "That's your problem."

That's living crazy!

Next-door neighbor: "Noah, what are you building?"
Noah: "An ark."
Next-door neighbor: "What's an ark?"
Noah: "I'm not sure."
Next-door neighbor: "What's it for?"
Noah: "For rain."
Next-door neighbor: "What's that? I've never heard of rain."
Noah: "Me either. But God says it's coming."

That's living crazy!

Gideon's chief-of-staff: "We're outnumbered 450 to 1. I hope you have a brilliant strategy. What's our battle plan, Captain?"
Gideon: "Arm each man with an empty jar, a torch, and a trumpet."
Gideon's chief-of-staff: "Wait . . . *what?*"
Gideon: "An empty jar, a torch, and a trumpet."
Gideon's chief-of-staff: "What are we going to do, have a garage sale?"
Gideon: "Actually, I thought we'd break the jars, then hold the torches up with one hand and play the trumpet with the other."
Gideon's chief-of-staff: "That's your battle plan?"
Gideon: "Yep."
Gideon's chief-of-staff: "You've *got* to be kidding."

That's living crazy!

Abraham didn't know where God was taking him or how God was going to make him a great nation. Noah didn't know what rain was. Gideon didn't know how his tiny group of men could defeat a massive army.

Uprooting your family, leaving everything familiar behind, and marching off into the desert without even knowing where you're going is crazy.

Spending seventy-five years building something you've never seen (an ark) in preparation for something else you've never seen (rain) is crazy.

Hoping that a rag-tag marching band busting glass and playing a tune will defeat a trained army of over one hundred thousand men is crazy.

But that's what Abraham, Noah, and Gideon did. They lived crazy. And God came through for them every single time.

God leading Abraham away from everything that was familiar and into the desert seemed like the worst thing that could happen. But it was a blessing in disguise. He was taking him to the Promised Land.

God ruining Noah's reputation and making him look like a fool seemed like the worst thing that could happen. But it was a blessing in disguise. He was saving Noah and his family's lives.

God whittling down Gideon's army to three hundred men and giving them a ridiculous battle plan seemed like the worst thing that could happen. But it was a blessing in disguise. He was setting the stage for one of the greatest victories of all time.

Sometimes the worst things that happen to us are actually the best. Sometimes we just need to live crazy.

***

Do you have enough faith to live crazy?

Let's be honest. This is an extremely unpopular and uncomfortable position. We're big fans of common sense, safety nets, and backup plans. We have an innate habit of trying to figure everything out, and of *needing* to figure everything out. We have to know our destination before we trot off into the desert. We have to have scientific proof of rain before we start preparing for it. And if we're outnumbered 450 to 1, we're not about to fight.

And it's all because we depend on ourselves instead of God, on our knowledge instead of His, on our ability instead of His power, and on our meager resources instead of His unlimited ones.

So maybe it's time for us to quit living like atheists. How's that for a realization?

Maybe it's time to abandon the safety nets. Maybe it's time to live crazy. Because if we're following God, we don't have to know the destination.

If we're following God, we don't have to see the rain. If we're following God, numbers don't matter!

These three men's names are etched into the Hall of Faith in Hebrews 11 because they exemplify what faith is, which is living with the same faith on both sides of the storm.

You don't have to be worried! You don't have to be afraid! If God is for us (and He is), and if He's working it all for our good (and He is), whom shall we fear?

***

Does everything about your Christian walk make sense? No. Is it logical? Probably not. If it is, then something is probably amiss.

When I read the Bible, there are very few things God calls people to do that make sense.

> God to Abraham: "Kill your only son."
> God to Joshua and the Israelites: "March around Jericho."
> God to Naaman: "Dip seven times in the Jordan river."
> God to Moses and the Israelites when Pharaoh's army is about to slaughter them: "Stand still."

"But that's the Old Testament," you say. "Things were different then."

Oh really? Jesus showed up in the New Testament and kept the living crazy theme going:

> "Untie that guy's donkey and bring it to me."
> "Feed these five thousand people."
> "I know he's expecting wine. But take this water to the governor."
> "Roll away the stone."

God doesn't call us to a life of safety. He doesn't call us to average and ordinary. He didn't save us so we could be normal. He calls us to live our lives beyond the simplicity of human reason. He calls us to a life of trust and a life of faith.

"Now faith is the substance of things hoped for, the evidence of things not seen."
(Hebrews 11:1)

"Living by faith" sounds really cute in a sermon. We nod and smile. But taking it out in the real world and actually *living* by faith? Not so cute. But faith isn't faith if it's based on circumstances. Faith is the evidence of things *not seen*.

We want everything to make sense. We want safety and security. We want everything to go according to our plan. We don't like surprises. We don't like unexpected changes. We want life to flow smoothly with our agenda, budget, and calendar. In fact, we want a God who makes it so we don't need a God. We want a God who removes all pain, confusion, and risks from life.

But why are we so afraid to take risks, when we serve the God of the universe?

Why are we scared to walk on water, when we serve the God who made it?

Because your problems only look big when your God looks small.

The second chapter of James tells us our actions are the proof of what we believe. So how do we act when God calls us to do something out of the ordinary? Do we panic every time a financial need arises? Are we overwhelmed with stress at the slightest problem? And if so, what does that say about our faith?

Anyone can have a good attitude when things are going well. Anyone can have peace when circumstances are peaceful. It's the Christian who should be calm when everything around them is falling apart. It's the Christian who should have peace in the midst of chaos. Because even when we don't know what tomorrow holds, we know Who holds tomorrow. And when our plans fall apart, His don't.

That's why I can say, "It is well," even when it seems like it isn't. That's why I can live crazy.

5

Redefining "Blessing"

If Moses had written his life, he wouldn't have written forty years in the desert. If Paul had written his life, he wouldn't have written a thorn in the flesh. And if Mary and Martha had written their life, they wouldn't have written a funeral.

In fact, Mary and Martha are totally devastated by the death of their brother Lazarus and they immediately call for Jesus. (That's always the best thing to do in times of crisis.)

Mary has it all figured out. She has carefully scripted the perfect solution to their circumstances. Jesus rushes in, heals Lazarus, then everyone high-fives and starts eating fried chicken. And they all live happily ever after.

But God didn't answer Mary's prayers. And God didn't follow Mary's plan because He had a better one.

Lazarus dies and Mary's plan goes up in smoke. Three days later when Jesus finally shows up, she is still gazing blankly at the dying embers of her plan, tears streaming down her face. All she can manage to say is, "Lord if you had been here, he wouldn't have died" (John 11:21).

This little statement is tinged with anger, sadness, grief, and frustration. And from it we learn two very important things about Mary.

First, it tells us that she had faith. She believed in Jesus. She believed in His power. But only in accordance with her plan. Which leads us to the second thing—her faith was limited.

She was boxing God in. And that was the problem. As long as Lazarus was still alive, she felt Jesus could use His miraculous power to heal him. But after he died, she apparently thought Jesus' miraculous power wasn't quite miraculous enough to make a difference. In essence, she believed things could turn out good, but only under a certain set of circumstances. And that set of circumstances was the little box she drew around God.

When Jesus asked if she believed, Mary responded, "*If* you had been here."

If—that's the key word. Our "ifs" are always an indication we are boxing God in.

Maybe you have an "if" of your own right now. "God, if this just wouldn't have happened . . ." "If this just would have gone a different direction . . ." "If you could've just met this need, or done this, or prevented this . . ."

You're standing there with your book, comparing it to God's book. And it doesn't match. It's the same thing Mary was doing because she was basically saying, "As long as my brother was alive, there was hope you could make something good out of this. And if you'd have followed my book and the way I would've written everything, it *would have* been good. But now that he's gone, there's no hope."

She was building a box of *if*.

Without realizing it, we often do the same thing. As long as God keeps our life within our little boxes, we're okay.

Trouble on the job might still fit inside our box. We still believe God can work it out. But what about when we unexpectedly get a pink slip? How could losing our job ever be a good thing? That's outside our box.

I've talked to so many people who, like Mary, fell into the trap of *if*. "If I hadn't lost my child . . ." "If I hadn't lost my job . . ."

"If I hadn't lost my loved one . . ." "If I just would've had good parents . . ." "If I just would've had this . . ." "If I just would've had that . . ." If, if, if . . .

But with three simple words, "Lazarus, come forth," Jesus reminded the world that God can't be boxed in. He recognized what Mary and Martha didn't—the fact that Lazarus died was a blessing.

They didn't see that. They were standing there crying and mourning. It's hard to blame them. We probably would've been doing the same thing. But get this—they were *mourning on the precipice of a miracle.* Without realizing it, they were mourning the greatest thing that ever happened to them.

Could it be that you and I are doing the same thing right now in certain areas of our lives? We mourn circumstances in our lives and say, "Man, I wish this was different . . ." "I wish this hadn't happened . . ." "I wish this *would* have happened . . ."

The beauty of Romans 8:28 is not just that God's going to wrap it up and work it for good. It's that this bad thing—this blessing in disguise—might be the *best thing* that could've happened to you!

On the Throne, Off the Throne

My friend, author and speaker Jim Laudell, puts a great perspective on how the events of our life affect our attitude towards God. He says if we're going to be honest and real, this is how it usually works:

We wake up Monday morning and think how grateful we are that we have a job and can make money to provide for our family.

God is on the throne.

But when we go to leave for work, we discover our truck has a flat tire.

What a lousy start to the day. I don't have time to fix this. I'm going to be late for work.

God's off the throne.

We decide to take the wife's car to work instead.

God's back on the throne!

We find out the in-laws are coming over this weekend. Oh joy.

God's back off the throne.

We decide to go hunting while the in-laws are in.

God's back on the throne!

The next week, the finances go bad. An unexpected bill leaves us stressed and worried.

God's off the throne.

The next day the boss gives us a raise. We pay the bill, and think, *Praise God, He's on the throne!*

No. Let me tell you something: He was on the throne the whole time! You just labeled it as bad because you weren't on the other side of it yet. But the good news is that you don't even have to be on the other side of it yet! This Romans 8:28 concept so thoroughly affects our lives that it changes the way we see *everything.*

When I walk out to my car and find a flat tire, I'm probably not going to click my heels together and whistle a tune. I'm going to be a little disappointed.

But how many stories have we heard of people having a flat tire or getting delayed in some way, only to discover a tragic car accident where they would have been had they been on time?

We may be grumbling about the very thing that could have been a life-saving mercy of God. We may be mourning a miracle.

So whatever it is that you're carrying today, and whatever burden or circumstance you have previously labeled as "bad," it could be that God has ordained for you to read this little book and discover that it's actually a blessing from Him.

He's on the throne when you're healthy. He's on the throne when you're not.

He's on the throne when finances are good. He's on the throne when finances are bad.

Keep that in mind when you stand, as Mary and Martha did, before the tombs of loss, bitterness, brokenness, and heartache. And be careful that you don't mourn a miracle.

With three simple words, Jesus turned Mary's tragedy into a triumph.

With three simple words, He turned her test into a testimony.

With three simple words, He revealed it was a blessing in disguise.

She thought it was the worst moment of life. It was actually the greatest.

***

What would you say if I asked you if you had a good week? How would you evaluate whether your week was good or not? How do you define *good*?

Does God bless us some weeks and not bless us other weeks? Or could it be that He blesses us every week and we simply define blessing as anything that fits our plan?

If I asked you what your blessings are, you would probably name things like your family, friends, and church. You would pick all the things that match your plan because that's how we define blessing—it's anything that fits our plan.

But my challenge to you is to redefine "blessing."

You'll discover that, while you still praise God for your blessings, you'll even begin to praise Him for your burdens!

Until I learned the beauty of Romans 8:28, I had never done that before. When I'd pray, I would praise Him for my blessings, and then spend the majority of my prayer time saying, "God you need to change this and do this and fix this . . . And this doesn't fit my plan . . . and this isn't the way I want it . . . ."

But it brings so much joy and freedom to realize that while the things that fit my plan are God's blessings, even the things that don't are going to work for my good. So they're a blessing, too! I can praise God for it all.

A Pain in the Back

I have unexplainable back trouble. My doctors don't know what caused it, but there has not been a day in four years that I can remember waking up without hurting. And like the lady in the Bible with the issue of blood, I've gone to many doctors and spent much money. And though I am grateful for a slight improvement, I am still in constant pain.

And here's the way my human mind works: *I'm young. I should be healthy. I shouldn't wake up every day with pain. If it hurts now, what's it going to do when I'm sixty?*

This back pain was not part of my plan. I didn't write in four years of pain and waking up hurting every morning. And this isn't a dramatic testimony with an emotional ending. I haven't been healed yet. The pain hasn't gone away yet. I'm still on this side of the storm.

I used to hate it. Every morning I'd wake up, feel the pain, and think, *God, I'm trying to live for you. I'm still young. Why is my back hurting?*

I'm not to the other side of this storm yet, and I don't know why God wrote this into my life. But after God pounded Romans 8:28 into my heart, it brought joy and peace into my life. As crazy as it sounds, now when I wake up each morning and feel the pain, instead of grimacing and being bitter, I say, "I don't know how this pain is a good thing, but I believe You meant what You said in Romans 8:28. So I thank You for this blessing and that You're going to work it for my good."

It's not an easy thing to do. But I believe Romans 8:28 with all my heart. And I believe that God is somehow going to work out my back pain for good.

I believe God can heal me, and maybe He will. But even if He doesn't, maybe I'll be a testimony through my pain. Maybe I'll simply learn to empathize with hurting people. I don't know the answer and I've quit trying to figure it out. But I know He has a purpose.

I certainly haven't mastered this yet. But I live differently now, because I know God's blessings don't just come in the form of things that fit my plan. Many times they come through pain, tears, and trials. Most of the time, my blessings come through things I didn't have planned.

I bet you have something in your life you wake up with every day. And until now, you may have considered it a burden, not a blessing. But I challenge you to redefine the term "blessing."

Now remember, we're not thanking God for the pain. We're thanking Him for what He's teaching us *through* the pain. We're not thanking God for the cancer. We're thanking God for the good He's going to work into our life *through* it.

***

I used to place everything in my life into two categories: good and bad. I would put everything that wasn't part of my plan, including my back pain, on one side. On the other side, I would put all the things I considered good—all the things that *were* part of my plan.

Then I would try to be spiritual and focus on the "good" side. I tried to be positive, thankful, and all that. But Romans 8:28 has radically changed my life, because now I realize that God is going to use all the things I put in the "bad" category for my good!

These days when I wake up and encounter those things, I can say, "This isn't in my book, God. But you're going to work it for good." I will never see my problems the same way again.

Integrating this truth into our life is a process, and it's one I haven't mastered. But it has changed my life, and it can do the same for you.

6

More Than Conquerors

After stating in Romans 8:28 that all things work together for good, Paul proceeds to give a nasty laundry list of every kind of problem imaginable. We're not talking hangnails and traffic delays here. This is heavy-hitting stuff.

Here's the picture he paints: famine (we have no food), nakedness (we have no clothes), peril (we are in life-threatening situations), and sword (somebody's trying to kill us).

And that's not even the complete list.

Now you and I may have had some bad days, but you probably have to think back pretty far to remember a time when you were starving and naked while someone was trying to kill you. *That's* a bad day.

So after painting this picture, Paul holds it up with eyes gleaming. And this is what he says:

" . . . in all these things we are more than conquerors . . . "
(Romans 8:37)

Did you catch it? It's a glorious little two-letter word that packs an omnipotent punch. It may be the greatest little two-letter sermon ever preached: *In* all these things.

I had always thought he meant "*in spite* of all these things." But the actual words Paul used in the original language carry the idea that it's not *in spite* of these things, but maybe even *because of them*, that we are conquerors.

It wasn't in spite of their brother's death, but *because of it*, that Mary and Martha were about to have the greatest moment of victory and conquering in their life.

The same was true of Joseph. It makes me love his story even more.

We spend all our time talking about when he's in the palace. When we think of Joseph, that's where we picture him. He's the emperor, second in command. He has a ton of power, all the nations are coming to him for food, and life is good. He's the man. He's in control. That's how we write the fairy tale story right there! There's not a single one of us who wouldn't want that.

But we often forget that the path to the palace led through the pit. And the pit wasn't part of Joseph's plan.

God had given Joseph a vision of his destiny. Joseph had a dream, and in his dream God said, "You're going to rule over your brothers. You're going to be the one that everyone comes to for resources." God was giving Joseph a glimpse of his destiny. *This is why I've created you; this is how I'm going to use you.*

But after Joseph glimpses the palace, God puts him in the pit.

Have you ever been there? I have.

We feel God's direction to start a business, or a relationship, or pursue a dream, or make a sacrifice . . . and then it seems like God slams all the doors and windows shut. The business fails, the relationship falls apart, and the dream dies.

I'd like to have a conversation with Joseph at the bottom of the pit. Can you imagine what was going through his mind?

"I'm going to rule over my brothers? They just stripped me and threw me in a well! I must have misheard God."

See, that's what we always do. Our first reaction is to doubt what God said. But Joseph hadn't misheard God. The pit was part of God's plan.

From Bad to Worse

Not only did the path to the palace lead through the pit—from there it lead to the prison!

After being dug out of the well, Joseph is sold into slavery. You know what he probably thought? *Oh, that's not good.*

But then he finds out he's headed to Egypt. Once there, God gives him favor. He does well and begins to rise through the ranks.

He thinks, "This is it! I passed the test in the pit, and now God's going to use me. He's going to help people through me. We're back on plan. Back on schedule."

Enter Potiphar's wife. Next thing Joseph knows, he's sitting in jail. And this wasn't a quick night in the county jail. He was there for over two years! In fact, twenty-two years passed between the time Joseph's brothers sold him into slavery until the time he ruled over them.

Let's pause right here for an important point: the delay of your dream is not the death of your dream. God's plan is right on track.

We can handle a day in the prison. Our faith is usually at least that strong. But the further things get from our plan, the longer it takes, the weaker our faith and stronger our doubt.

Day one: "God's setting the stage for a miracle!"

Day two: "Well . . . I thought He was setting the stage for a miracle."

Day three: "I think I'm confused."

Maybe you're in the pit or the prison right now in your life. Things are getting further from the plan you had all laid out. For a while, you held out hope that God would get things back on course. But now your plan is totally gone and you have no idea what God is doing.

Let me tell you what He's doing: He's taking you places.

Don't forget the vision He's given you. Because it doesn't matter what's between here and there. God's going to work it all for good.

That's why we can smile on *this* side of the storm. I don't have to wait for the stone to roll away and Lazarus to come out. I know God's going to work it out!

I can smile and go about my business in the prison, because I know I wasn't made for the prison. I was made for the palace.

I am a conqueror. Not just in spite of my challenges. But because of them.

7

The Weight of Worry

The need to know how everything's going to work out is a heavy weight. And I challenge you to drop it. You were never made to carry it. God never intended for you to know how everything would happen. He intended for you to trust Him enough to truly believe Romans 8:28. He intended for you to have the constant peace of knowing *all things work together for good.*

We've all carried the weight of worry at some point. *What's going to happen when my kids get older? How am I going to pay this bill? How is this going to work out? How will I ever meet the right person? What if I lose my job? What about the economy?*

Our human nature is such that we are addicted to the weight of worry. And over and over, I find myself picking it up again. God has to constantly tap me on the shoulder and say, "I didn't create you to carry that. Cast your care upon me."

Truth is, if we could truly wrap our mind around Romans 8:28 and grasp this concept, we would be the freest, happiest, most liberated people in the world.

Do you realize how joyful your life could be? When your happiness is rooted in circumstances, you are at the mercy of those circumstances. But when you know God is working *every single tiny detail* of your life for your good, circumstances no longer matter! You can live in victory. You can live in joy. You can live in peace.

Get thrown in a well? Hey, God's in control!
Get sold into slavery? Hey, God's taking me to the palace!
Get thrown in prison? Hey, it's all part of His plan!
Have a flat tire? He spared me from a wreck!
Lose a job? He's got a better one lined up for me!

You can spend your life bemoaning your burdens. Or you can spend it rejoicing in the knowledge that they are blessings in disguise.

David learned this and he said,

"It is good for me that I have been afflicted . . . "
(Psalm 119:71)

Now this is another statement that sounds crazy. Come on. Really, when was the last time something bad happened to you and you reacted with, "Praise God! That was good!"

That sounds ludicrous. But David knew God was working it for good. And he probably would've agreed with Sir Thomas Browne, who thousands of years later, wrote, "We should not quarrel rashly with adversities not yet understood, nor overlook the mercies often bound up in them, for we consider not sufficiently the good of evil, nor fairly compute the mercies of Providence in things afflictive at first hand."

***

Think about it: why do you get angry? Because things don't go the way you want.

Why do you get discouraged? Every time you've ever been discouraged in your life, it was because things don't go the way you wanted.

Why do you get frustrated? Because things aren't the way you want them to be.

Today you may look at some of your circumstances and respond with sorrow and discouragement. But if you only knew . . .

If God took you to heaven and showed you true perspective, you would immediately rejoice and praise God for your "problems."

I know that's a shift. I know that's a little unnatural and uncomfortable. (Okay, very unnatural and very uncomfortable.) But it's the truth.

I think James was laughing when he told us to count it all joy when we encounter trials and tribulations (James 1:2). That's crazy! But the original language literally means, "Get excited when bad things happen."

Why? Because it's a blessing in disguise! It's God pouring grace and good things into your life.

Can you imagine if we all took this idea and lived it out? When we had relationship troubles, instead of being depressed, we'd cry out, "Thank you, God, that You're working on us. Thank You that You care enough about us to stress us."

Stress creates strength. In fact, the only way you can get strength is through stress.

When you exercise, it literally stresses your muscle and tears it apart. It breaks it. But this brokenness you are left with is not the end of the story, because the healing process builds the muscle back even stronger than before. In fact, the tear in a muscle or the break in a bone becomes the strongest part when it heals.

Your muscles can't grow without stress. And neither can your relationships.

If God took all the problems out of your life and wrote it according to your plan, you would be the weakest person in the world.

Can you hear the cry of God's heart? "I am strengthening you. I have put this pain and these problems into your life for a specific purpose. I'm in total control. These things aren't to destroy you; they're to strengthen you. I knew you before you were born and I'm working every detail of your life for your good. Every phone call, every text message, every relationship, every church service, every accident, every conversation, every person you meet, every opportunity you encounter . . . *every single thing in your life* is in my control, and I'm weaving them all together for your good. I know exactly what I'm doing!"

8

What You Need
More Than Anything

There is one thing in this world that you need more than anything. More than a new car. More than good health. More than a better job. You may need to lose weight or finish your degree. But you need this more. Way more.

What you need more than anything is to learn more about God.

I know, I know. That sounds preachy. But don't be fooled by the simplicity of that statement. Sometimes the simplest things are the most powerful.

When I say, "learning more about God," I don't just mean facts and information. We have a word for people who know lots of information about someone without having a relationship with them: stalker.

I'm talking about learning *Who* God really is. I'm talking about experiencing Him and discovering more of Him. The more you learn of God, the more you'll realize how little of Him you know.

***

The northern portion of Africa is covered in 3.5 million square miles of sweltering desert called the Sahara. It's the largest desert in the world and is similar in size to the United States.

So imagine walking to the edge of the Sahara and scooping up a handful of dry sand. Now imagine letting the sand run through your fingers until only a single grain remained. It rests on your fingertip, and it is so tiny you can barely see it.

What if I told you your entire knowledge and concept of God was equal to that little grain of sand, while the 3.5 million square miles of sand in front of you represented the endless and incomprehensible depths of who He really is?

"O the depth of the riches
both of the wisdom and knowledge of God!
how unsearchable are his judgments, and his ways past finding out!"
(Romans 11:33)

God longs for us to know more of Him. It saddens His heart when we settle for a single grain of sand when He longs to show us the astounding depths of His love. He longs to dazzle us with His power, and comfort us with His compassion.

He wants us to feel His glory and experience His presence. When we experience God in this way, we are so full that we desire nothing else. God is the only all-satisfying good.

He created us to need Him, and He created everything in our life to be directly affected by our knowledge of Him.

That's why our greatest need is the need to learn more of God. And because God cares so deeply about us, He longs to meet that greatest need.

So what does all this have to do with bad circumstances in our lives?

Our knowledge of God is one of the most important things in our life. Where does this knowledge come from? From our burdens. Bad circumstances are often what teach us about God. It is because of sorrow that we learn God can comfort. It is because of a broken heart that we learn God can mend one. It is because of needs that we learn God can provide. It is because of our failures that we learn of God's forgiveness.

These things, though unpleasant, are teaching us about God. They are meeting the greatest need in our life.

***

Some dear friends were expecting a child a few years ago. When their son Aaron was born, there were many complications with his health. After several days of struggle in this world, and despite the prayers of many friends and family members, he passed away.

A few days later, his mother was working through her grief and pouring her heart out to God in prayer. She was a strong woman of faith, and was even scheduled to speak at a women's retreat the next week. But as you can imagine, the grief was indescribably painful.

She would never get to watch him grow up. She'd never teach him to ride his bike. She'd never watch him blow out the candles on his birthday cake.

He had a unique personality but she'd never get to see it. He had talents but she'd never know what they were.

"I didn't even get to know him!" she cried to God.

He immediately spoke to her heart, "I didn't send him so you'd get to know him. I sent him so you'd get to know Me."

God is constantly orchestrating all the events of our lives with a single ultimate goal in mind: He wants us to know Him.

God's sweetest mercies and richest blessings are His actions that give us what we most need. And what we most need is to draw closer to Him. And what causes us to draw closer to Him is usually the pain and problems in our life.

Like the waves of the ocean wash away the sand covering hidden treasure, so the waves of our problems often reveal the buried treasure of God's greatness.

Needs Versus Wants

God is more interested in giving you what you need, than giving you what you want.

What we want is more money in the bank. What we want is good health. What we want is perfect relationships. What we want is sunshine and smooth sailing.

But God's so much smarter than we are.

God's greatest blessings are the waves that crash us against the Rock of Ages, the droughts that lead us to the Water of Life, and the wolves that chase us back to the Shepherd.

If God is our greatest good, then what makes something good is whether it brings us more of God.

Look back over your life. When were the times when God was really there? When were the best spiritual moments of your life?

You're probably not going to say, "You know, I remember when money was in the bank and everything was going good, relationships were great, everybody was healthy . . . and God really did something in my heart."

No, it's in the sleepless nights. It's in the hospitals. It's in the pain, problems, and processes that we don't like.

We want good qualities in our life. But we don't want the problems and pain that produce those qualities.

We want patience. But we don't want to have to stand in line to learn it or be subject to the trying of our faith that produces it.

We want joy. But we don't want the sorrow that teaches us to appreciate it.

We want to see God meet our needs. But we'd rather not have any needs to begin with.

We want to see miracles. But we don't want to need them.

We love God's strength. But we don't like that it is made perfect in our weakness.

We like watching the Red Sea roll back. But we don't like being cornered in front of it with an army galloping toward us.

The Ultimate Perspective

I believe when we get to heaven and have the ability to look back over our life and see what God was doing, it's going to blow our mind. I don't know how everything will work, but I think God will let us look back on our life and see His glory. And the moment we step into eternity and have perfect vision, I think we're going to buckle to our knees.

For the first time, with full comprehension, we will understand everything God was doing. And we will cry, "God, you were so good! I didn't realize what You were doing, but You were doing it for my good."

With tears streaming down my cheeks, I will fall to my knees and say, "God, I didn't realize why my back was hurting every morning, but now I see! It was for Your glory. It was good; it was a blessing."

We won't look back at our lives and see some good circumstances and some bad circumstances. We'll realize it was *all* a blessing. He was working it all for good.

***

God wants to change your definition of "blessing." He wants you to wake up with joy, no matter what happens. He wants you to rest and trust in Him, knowing that He's in control. And He wants you to realize He's placed those problems you're battling and growing bitter against in your life to help you.

That's what He's taught me. It's been hard, and I'm a slow learner. But it has brought so much joy and perspective to my life. And I think it will do the same thing for you.

Envision those things you've labeled bad: The thing you wish wasn't in your life, the person you wish wasn't in your life, the situation you wish wasn't in your life. Would you give those things to God? Would you let Him take those ashes and make beauty out of it?

He may not explain to you how it's all going to work. He may not reveal His plan, or explain His reasons. But that's the whole point. You don't have to know. You don't have to see. You don't have to understand. All you have to do is trust that He will weave any misery into sweet music. He knows what He's doing.

God is the great conductor of this orchestra called life. And not a note is played without His permission. To us, the melody of life seems to be off key at times, the rhythm a bit off-beat. We question the Conductor and fear He has lost control. But every note is carefully directed, every harmony intricately purposed.

And it will only be at the end of the symphony, when the thunderous applause of heaven fills the hall, that we will appreciate the beauty of the music, and the genius of the Conductor.

So trust Him. Rest. Breathe. Let go. He knows what He's doing.

The wonderful things in your life are blessings.

And the not-so-wonderful things? Well, they're blessings, too. They're just blessings in disguise.

Acknowledgements

Who deserves the credit for a delicious meal? The one who cooked it? The one who made the recipe? The one who grew the ingredients? The truth is, they all do.

I typed the words. But these people made the meal possible:

- My sweet wife Alicia, my best friend in this world. I love you.
- My parents, who believed in my dreams, but taught me character is the greatest success. A son could not ask for more.
- My three sisters, whose love and encouragement made me believe I could actually do this. They are princesses.
- My fellow literary entrepreneur, Jim Laudell, whose encouragement, initiative, and passion constantly inspire me.
- My editor, Alice Sullivan, whose sarcasm makes me laugh out loud. She can do to a manuscript what Michelangelo did to the Sistine Chapel.
- My designer, Zoran Kochoski, for creating a cover no one could forget.
- My friend, Erica McNeal, not only for writing the foreword to this book, but for inspiring me with her life and testimony.
- And most of all, to God, who makes all things possible. All the glory belongs to Him.

About the Author

Joshua M. Hood is a sinner saved by grace. He's also a Christian author, speaker, and average golfer. His writings have been featured on top-ranked sites including pastors.com and michaelhyatt.com, and have reached over a quarter of a million people in over 170 of the world's 196 countries.

He lives in North East Texas with his sweet wife Alicia.

You can find out more about him at joshuamhood.com. To have him speak at your church or event: joshuamhood.com/speaking.

You can also connect with him here:
Twitter: @JoshuaMHood
Facebook: facebook.com/joshuamhood

Made in the USA
Lexington, KY
22 May 2017